THE DAY JESUS DIED

Matthew 26:47–27:66; Mark 14:43–15:47;
Luke 22:47–23:56; and John 18:1–19:42 for children

Written by Bryan Davis
Illustrated by Ron Gordon

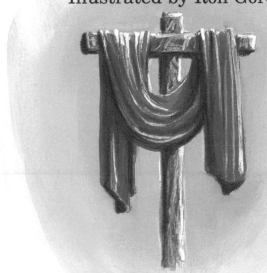

Arch® Books
Copyright © 1998 Concordia Publishing House
3558 S. Jefferson Avenue, St. Louis, MO 63118-3968
Printed in Colombia

When Jesus was with us on earth long ago,
He suffered and died in our place.
The story is sad but important because
It speaks to the whole human race.

It happened according to God's holy plan;
It was no mistake, not at all.
Beginning one night when He knelt down to pray,
Obeying, He followed God's call.

He said, "Oh, My Father, We're one, it is true.
Please help My disciples to know
That they should be one even after I die.
Now, Father, I'm ready to go."

Then after He rose, a crowd came and grabbed Him
As Judas kissed our Lord's cheek.
They took Him to trial in the city that night, but
The priests could not get Him to speak.

They marched Him to Pilate who asked,
    "Then shall I
Release this man, King of the Jews?"
The people said, "No. You must give us Barabbas."
Those priests told the crowd to refuse.

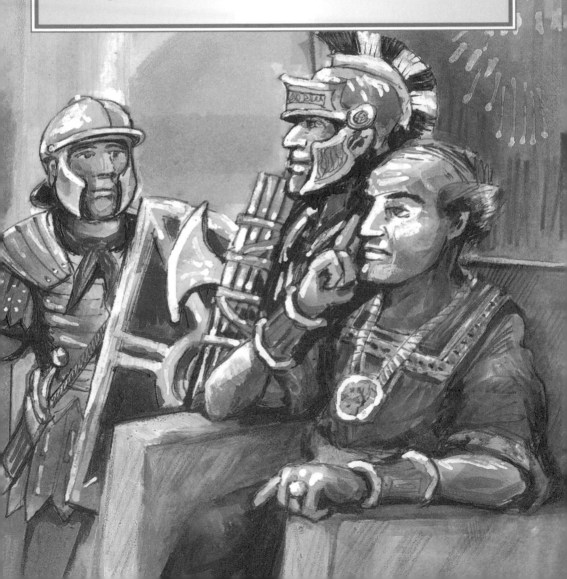

So Jesus was beaten and sentenced to die;
The pain was all part of God's will.
A crown made of thorns was pushed onto His head.
He dragged a big cross up a hill.

They nailed up His hands on that old rugged cross;
His feet were both fastened there too.
A few of His friends made their way to the hill,
But what could these frightened ones do?

"Forgive them, My Father!" He cried out in pain.
"They truly do not understand."
For how could they know He was dying to save?
'Twas all in the Father's great plan.

The soldiers all mocked Him by kneeling and bowing.
They spat and said, "Hail, Jewish king!"
They picked up His shirt and then gambled to win it.
Their hate was a terrible thing.

Two robbers were crucified with Him that day.
And one said, "If You are the Lord,
Just rescue Yourself and then get us all down."
He laughed with the loud, mocking horde.

The other said, "What? Don't you even fear God?
We're guilty, but He is not so."
He said to the Lord, "Please remember me when
Up to Your great kingdom You go."

Then Jesus said, "Yes, you will be with Me there,"
As darkness came over the sky.
It lasted three hours while our sins fell upon Him.
The people could not explain why.

Then Jesus cried out, "My God, oh My God!
Why have You forsaken Your Son?"
They thought He had called out for help from Elijah
And guessed that the prophet might come.

"I thirst," Jesus called as His death drew much closer.
He must now fulfill the last sign.
"Let's give Him a drink!" a man yelled while running.
He lifted a sponge filled with wine.

"And now it is finished," our Lord cried with a gasp.
Then Jesus drew in His last breath.
"My Father, My spirit I put into Your hands."
And bowing, He passed into death.

A soldier then pierced the Lord's side with a spear.
He had to make sure He was dead.
Then Joseph came up with his friend Nicodemus.
They wrapped up His body and head.

They laid His dead body down in a new tomb
And rolled a big stone in the way.
But death couldn't keep our Lord down in the grave.
He rose again on the third day.

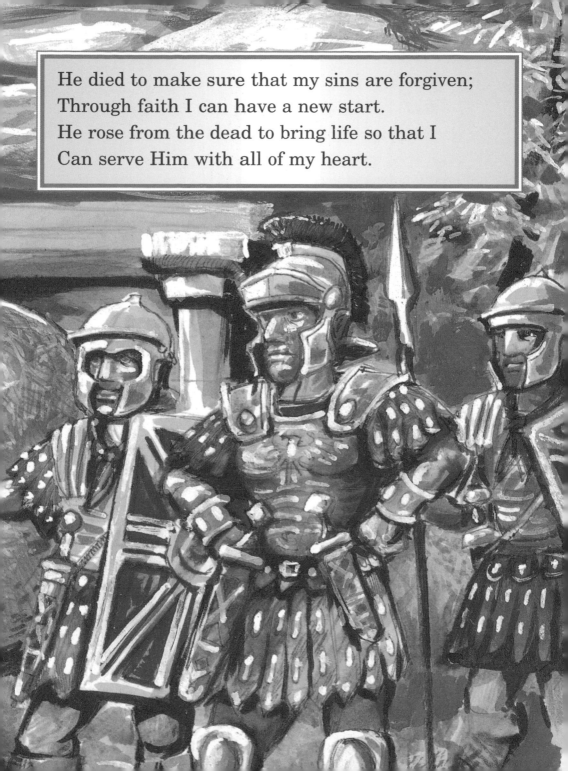

He died to make sure that my sins are forgiven;
Through faith I can have a new start.
He rose from the dead to bring life so that I
Can serve Him with all of my heart.

Dear Parents:

The story of Jesus' crucifixion is a difficult one for very young children to understand. Hopefully such physical anguish is not a part of their world. Place a simple cross on your kitchen table or at some other focal point in your home. Explain to your child that Jesus loves us so much, He died on the cross to take the punishment for the things we do wrong. A cross reminds us of how much Jesus loves us.

Look for crosses when you go to church next Sunday. Look for crosses in the world around you—a necklace, the cross beam of a telephone pole, the letter "t," etc. Each time your child finds a cross, say a simple prayer to Jesus, thanking Him for His love.

The Editor